A *DISCIPLESHIP JOURNAL* BIBLE • STUDY ON
RELATIONSHIPS

BUILDING BETTER RELATIONSHIPS

BY SUSAN NIKAIDO

NAVPRESS ◑
P.O. Box 35001, Colorado Springs, Colorado 80935

OUR GUARANTEE TO YOU

The Navigators is an international Christian organization. Our mission is to reach, disciple, and equip people to know Christ and to make Him known through successive generations. We envision multitudes of diverse people in the United States and every other nation who have a passionate love for Christ, live a lifestyle of sharing Christ's love, and multiply spiritual laborers among those without Christ.

NavPress is the publishing ministry of The Navigators. NavPress publications help believers learn biblical truth and apply what they learn to their lives and ministries. Our mission is to stimulate spiritual formation among our readers.

Cover Illustration: Kari Alberg
Cover Design: Steve Eames and Dan Jamison
Creative Team: Eric Stanford, Marla Kennedy, Lori Mitchell, Vickie Howard

Printed in the United States of America

1 2 3 4 5 6 7 8 9 10 11 12 13 14 15 / 04 03 02 01 00

Contents

Introduction

Growing Stronger Relationships

Relationships can bring us more joy than anything else in life . . . and also more pain. When they're going well, they bring us the support, affirmation, and joyful companionship that keep us going and make life worth living. When they're not, everything in our lives can seem out of kilter.

How we respond to the people around us—from those we love to those we sometimes wish would just go away—is also a testing ground for our commitment to Christ. Jesus said the second greatest commandment is to "love your neighbor as yourself" (Mark 12:31). He also said the world will know whether we follow Him by observing the way we relate to other believers (John 13:34-35).

Over the years, *Discipleship Journal* has published a number of articles about relationships. This study compiles some of those significant articles and combines them with discussion questions and innovative learning activities that can help you become more like Jesus in the way you relate to the people around you.

As you interact with the articles, questions, and activities, you'll examine the following questions about building better relationships:

- What does it mean to love others?
- How does humility—or the lack of it—affect my relationships? Are there any blind spots of pride in my life?
- What is true fellowship? How can I develop the kind of rich relationships God intended among believers?
- How can I build deeper friendships?

- How can I forgive the people who have hurt me?
- What should I do when conflict arises?
- What if conflict cannot be resolved?

How This Study Guide Works

This *Discipleship Journal* Bible study may look a little different from study guides you have used in the past. In addition to the Scripture that you'll be looking at in each article, we've combed through issues of *Discipleship Journal* magazine and selected some of the best articles on a variety of topics essential to living life as a disciple of Christ in today's world.

This combination of Scripture texts and the sharpened insights of experienced communicators should give you plenty to contemplate as you discover what it means to follow Jesus in your life situation. The idea is to help you to be a "doer" of the Word and not merely a "hearer" (James 1:22, NRSV).

Not all questions incorporate specific verses of Scripture, but they all are intended to help you think through what it means to apply biblical truth. Sometimes that will involve changing the way you *think*, and often it will mean changing the way you *act*.

This study guide is designed to be used either individually or in a small-group setting. (Your experience will likely be enhanced by the input, perspective, and prayers of like-minded believers.) Even if you work on this study on your own, we encourage you to share your insights and discoveries with someone who can help "sharpen" you in your walk with God (see Proverbs 27:17).

Our prayer is that God's Word will both challenge and encourage you as you seek to follow Him "with all your heart and with all your soul and with all your mind and with all your strength" (Mark 12:30).

Learning to Love, Part I

"If I have not love, I am nothing," Paul wrote in 1 Corinthians 13:2. Jesus said that the second greatest commandment, after loving God, is loving people. Indeed, if we "live a life of love" as God desires (Ephesians 5:2), we will naturally obey most of His other commands.

To build better relationships, we need first and foremost to become better "lovers." In the following article entitled "**How Do You Love?**" **by J. Oswald Sanders** (excerpted from Issue 2), the author discusses a familiar Bible passage that gives us a picture of the "life of love" to which we are called.

We will be examining this article in both sessions one and two. As you work through this study and the ones that follow, you may find it works best to read the article once without stopping to answer the questions. Underline any portions that stand out to you. Then read the article a second time, responding to the questions and exercises as you go.

1. In the space below, write the names of several people whom you'd like to love better. They can be people close to you or people you find difficult to love. Keep them in mind as you read the article and answer the questions.

The Love Chapter

Many years ago my wife and I decided to read 1 Corinthians 13 every day for a month. Every night when we went to bed we would either read it individually or recite it together.

After a week, the beauty of the chapter gripped us more than ever. But after the second week, reading it was getting decidedly awkward. And by the end of the third week, I was quite sure it was *not* a very beautiful chapter. For I would find myself during the day with attitudes in which love was absent, and immediately this chapter would speak to me, challenging my life on many counts.

The qualities of love attributed therein are a picture of the Lord Jesus. Everything said here was exactly true of Him. Jesus was patient. He was always kind. He was never jealous, never boastful, never arrogant or rude. Jesus never insisted on His own way. He was not irritable. He was not resentful. He never rejoiced at anything wrong; He always rejoiced in what was right. Jesus bore all things, believed all things, hoped all things, endured all things. Jesus never failed.

But let me put it another way, and see if you can follow: I am always patient and kind. I'm never jealous. I never boast. I'm never proud. I'm never rude. I never insist on having my own way. I'm never irritable. I'm never resentful. I never rejoice in anything wrong, and I always rejoice in what is right. I bear all things, I believe all things, I hope all things, I endure all things. I never fail.

Quite a difference, isn't there?

The word *love* as it is used today in literature and movies and on television is being sadly debased. Its connections are mostly with the romantic and the erotic. But in the Bible we see love as the sacrificial, self-imparting quality of God's nature. Did God so love the world that He felt a warm glow in His heart? No, God so loved the world that He plucked out His heart and gave His only Son. That's the kind of love spoken of in 1 Corinthians 13.

2. Choose and read one of the following chapters from the Gospels: Matthew 9, Mark 10, Luke 7, or John 14. In the space below, write down all that you observe from this chapter about the way Jesus loved people.

3. What is it about Jesus' love that stands out to you the most?

4. a. Read 1 John 4:7-12,16-17,19-21, printed below. Underline all the statements that indicate why it is important that we love one another.

Dear friends, let us love one another, for love comes from God. Everyone who loves has been born of God and knows God. Whoever does not love does not know God, because God is love. This is how God showed his love among us: He sent his one and only Son into the world that we might live through him. This is love: not that we loved God, but that he loved us and sent his Son as an atoning sacrifice for our sins.

Dear friends, since God so loved us, we also ought to love one another. No one has ever seen God; but if we love one another, God lives in us and his love is made complete in us. . . .

God is love. Whoever lives in love lives in God, and God in him. In this way, love is made complete among us so that we will have confidence on the day of judgment, because in this world we are like him. . . .

We love because he first loved us. If anyone says, "I love God," yet hates his brother, he is a liar. For anyone who

*does not love his brother, whom he has seen, cannot love
God, whom he has not seen. And he has given us this command: Whoever loves God must also love his brother.*

   b. From this passage in 1 John, summarize why it is so impor-
      tant to God that we love the people around us.

The Supremacy of Love

In the first three verses of 1 Corinthians 13, Paul showed the
supremacy of love over other things. Love has supremacy over spiritual gifts. Paul said he could have ecstatic utterances and wonderful
rhetoric, but if he had not love he was like the noisy gong they
could hear sounding in the heathen temples. A spiritual gift is of
value only as it is prompted by and exercised in love.

Paul said love has supremacy over intellectual powers. He said
if he had prophetic powers and understood all mysteries and all
knowledge, and if he had all faith so as to remove mountains, but
had not love, he was *nothing.*

He went further. Love has supremacy over material sacrifice.
You can dole out all your goods to feed the poor until you have
nothing left. Yet all the money you've given isn't entered to your
credit in heaven unless your giving is motivated by love.

These absolutes stated by Paul are devastating. If you or I had
written that second verse, we would have said, "If you have
prophetic powers, if you understand all mysteries and all knowledge,
if you have all faith, and yet you don't have love, you won't be nearly
as effective as you otherwise would be." But Paul said you can know
your Bible backwards and forwards, yet without love you are nothing. You can have the kind of faith that gets wonderful answers to
prayer, but if you don't have love you are a spiritual nobody.

Paul wasn't trying to denigrate spiritual gifts or knowledge or
having the faith that moves mountains. But he said all these things
must be motivated by love or they are spiritually barren.

5. How do you react to Paul's statement that spiritual gifts, knowledge, mountain-moving faith, sacrificial giving, and even dying for your faith amount to *nothing* if you are not a loving person?

The Look of Love

First Corinthians 13:4-8 contains a personified list of love's qualities. The first is patience. People are not always easy to be patient with, are they? But love is capable of great self-restraint.

Peter came to the Lord one day, perhaps after the other apostles had been giving Peter a rough time. He said, "Lord, how often should my brethren sin against me, and I forgive them? Seven times?"

I suppose he thought he'd made a great concession to forgive them seven times, but what did the Lord answer? Yes, Peter, that's wonderful to forgive them seven times, but I suggest that you try seventy times seven, and then come and see Me again. Seventy times seven!

How patient am I? How many times do I forgive someone who does something wrong? How many times do I get impatient with my children? Love is patient—and when I am impatient, it's because there's a shortage of love.

6. With whom are you most likely to get impatient? Check all that apply.

☐ Your children
☐ Your spouse
☐ Other family members
☐ People to whom you are ministering

11

☐ Inconsiderate people
☐ People who do things slowly
☐ People who repeatedly make mistakes
☐ Other (describe):

7. How do you generally treat people when you are impatient?

8. Think of a person or situation that often tries your patience. How could having a loving attitude give you the ability to be more patient with this person or situation?

D Love is kind. A kind person is someone who is always looking out for opportunities to do something good for others. In Acts 10:38, Peter spoke about the Lord Jesus being anointed "with the Holy Spirit and power." What was the effect of this anointing? Does the passage say Jesus went about preaching wonderful sermons and doing great miracles? No, it says, "He went around *doing good*" (emphasis added). He looked for opportunities to help people.

Kindness is putting yourself at the disposal of other people, forgetting and losing yourself in their interests, trying to help them and make them happy. Love is just like that.

9. Describe a time when you observed someone showing kindness, either in word or in deed.

10. Why is kindness a sign of love?

11. Read 1 Thessalonians 5:15 and 2 Timothy 2:24. In what kinds of situations does Paul tell us to be kind?

12. Is there anyone with whom you are currently having a conflict or who has recently hurt you? If so, what would it look like to show kindness to that person?

13. Read Jeremiah 9:24. How does God respond when we show kindness to others?

D Love is never jealous, never envious. Love never envies someone who is more gifted, more attractive, or more successful, someone who is richer or owns more, or who is more clever. Isn't it part of our nature to say, "I wish I had that"? Doesn't our culture play upon this covetous streak in us and make us envy what others have, so that we want something better all the time? But love is content with what it has. Love is content with what God has given, in personality or possessions or in anything else.

I think of John the Baptist as one of the most remarkable examples of a man without jealousy. He had been the center of the Jewish nation's attention. He went out to the desert and the crowds followed him there from every direction. Then Jesus came on the scene, and John found his followers leaving him and going after Jesus. He found his congregation going to the church around the corner, so to speak.

What was John's reaction? He said, "My joy is fulfilled. I love to hear the Bridegroom's voice and I'm listening to it now. He must increase and I must decrease." Love is not jealous.

14. In which of the following areas are you most easily tempted to envy others? Check any that apply.

☐ Possessions
☐ Looks
☐ Career
☐ Spouse
☐ Talents
☐ Relationships
☐ Self-confidence
☐ Children's achievements
☐ Other (describe):

15. Why is envy inconsistent with love?

16. Read Romans 12:15. What did Paul say our attitude is to be when good things happen to others?

17. Consider the following qualities of love described thus far in the article. Put a star by the one you feel is strongest in your life. Place a check mark next to the area in which you'd most like to grow.

__ Patient

__ Kind

__ Never jealous

18. What do you feel God has been saying to you through this study about the way you love?

19. Choose one of the people you listed in question one at the beginning of this session. What changes could you make this week in order to love that person better?

Parting Thought
If love is the greatest command, then unloving, selfish, or hateful acts would be among the greatest of sins.
—Anne L. Meskey, "What's the Big Deal About Love?" Issue 79

2

Learning to Love, Part 2

In session one we learned that love is patient, kind, and not envious, and we thought through some of the implications of those qualities for our own lives. Now, as we continue to read "**How Do You Love?**" **by J. Oswald Sanders,** we will examine still more qualities of love, such as being humble, encouraging, and constant, not irritable or resentful. A key factor in getting the most out of this session is being open to recognizing the areas where we could love others better.

Putting Others First

Love is not proud—arrogant, puffed up, conceited, self-important. Who of us is not proud? Pride seems inborn with us. It is like an onion: You take off one skin and you come to another, then another still—and all the while it makes you cry. Pride is an abomination to the Lord. He will abase the proud and exalt the humble [James 4:6]. The only person who ever trod this earth who had the right to be proud was not, but instead "humbled himself and became obedient to death—even death on a cross" (Philippians 2:8).

Humility is not something which grows as a native plant in my life or in yours, but is exotic. It comes down from heaven, implanted in our lives by the Holy Spirit. [Session three will focus on having this humility in our relationships.]

Love is not rude. There is an etiquette in the Christian life, and love doesn't forget it. I don't think as much emphasis is given to manners today as in the past, and we've lost something by it. Love is never crude, never sarcastic, never vulgar.

Love does not insist on its own way. Yet for you and me to seek our own interests is as natural as breathing. This is especially disruptive in our homes, when one family member or another insists on having his way. Paul cried out, "Everyone looks out for his own interests, not those of Jesus Christ" (Philippians 2:21).

One of the marks of spiritual maturity is being able to give in graciously in the ordinary things of life. In Ephesians 5:18 we are commanded to be filled with the Spirit. Three verses later we read, "Submit to one another." This submission is a mark of being Spirit-controlled.

Learning to be mutually submissive and mutually willing to give way to another will make the wheels run more smoothly in a home or in any group or community. In the interest of harmony, love doesn't even insist on its rights.

1. How does insisting on our own way damage relationships?

2. List several kinds of situations in which believers sometimes insist on having things their way.

   ▪ In the home:

   ▪ In the church:

3. In which areas are you most often tempted to insist on having your own way?

18

4. Are there times when you think God would prefer that we make the "wrong" decision—that is, choose an option that seems less efficient or effective—in the name of love? If so, give one or two examples.

5. Are there any situations in which we *should* insist on the course of action we want? If so, in what kinds of situations?

D Love is not easily provoked or angered. Love is not irritable. Love does not get exasperated or lose its temper. Do you have your times of irritability? When you come to breakfast in the morning does the rest of the family look to see which way the wind is blowing today?

6. Under what conditions do you tend to be irritable?

☐ Busyness
☐ Work pressures
☐ Tiredness or lack of sleep
☐ Hormonal fluctuations
☐ Unresolved conflict
☐ Other (describe):

7. How do you tend to respond to people when you're feeling irritable?

8. When you're feeling irritable, what would most help you
    avoid responding unkindly to others?

    ☐ Stop and pray.
    ☐ Spend time meditating on Scripture.
    ☐ Find the root cause of your irritability and ask God to help
      you resolve it.
    ☐ Choose a loving response.
    ☐ Other (describe):

Love is not resentful. It keeps no record of wrongs. Love forgives and forgets. When I was a boy, a man in our church had a notebook in which he recorded wrong things that we young fellows did and said. Then later, at a very awkward time, out would come the book and we would be confronted with what we had done.

Years later I mentioned this when I was preaching one morning. I said love doesn't do that, since love keeps no record of wrongs. Love forgets.

After the service I was walking home with a friend and his young son. The boy spoke up, "Daddy, if Mr. Sanders had been doing what he preached about this morning, he wouldn't have remembered that man keeping that little book, would he?" He was right. Love forgets. (I'm remembering it now just to tell you!)

Is there some resentment in your heart against someone? In the back of your mind do you remember something that was done to you that you have never forgiven and put away? Resentment, like jealousy, is a cancer of the soul. It can only harm you. If you have resentment, I plead with you to forgive the person. How wonderfully God has forgiven us! Let us be just as forgiving. [In session six, we will examine forgiveness in greater depth.]

Love bears all things—it is "slow to expose," it always covers up, always protects. When you do something out of order, don't you appreciate it when no one talks about it—when they're silent and just pass it over? And yet how easy it is for us to talk about the mistakes of others. But love knows how to be silent. If this aspect of love was in the heart of each of us, we would know a wonderful warmth of fellowship, much deeper than we experience now.

9. In "Gossip: Holding Tongue in Check" (Issue 44), Carole Mayhall quotes 1 Corinthians 13:7 in *The Living Bible:* "If you love someone, you will be loyal to him no matter what the cost. You will always believe in him, always expect the best of him, and always stand your ground in defending him." Then she writes, "Am I believing, thinking, and saying the best about everyone I talk about? It seems to me that gossip and love are totally incompatible." How does love prevent gossip?

10. Gossip harms more than just the person being discussed. Read Ephesians 4:29. How does gossip show a lack of love for those who listen to it?

11. Look again at Ephesians 4:29. When we need to discuss what is going on in other people's lives, what guidelines should we follow?

Love believes all things and hopes all things. Love is always optimistic about its object. Love hopes the best. Love also endures all things—it can stand anything.

12. Sanders writes, "Love is always optimistic about its object." Think of someone who believed in you—someone who let you know he or she thought you could accomplish great things or become a better person. Who was it, and what impact did that person have on your life?

13. Are there some individuals you could encourage this week by telling them that you believe in them? List their names and how you plan to encourage them.

14. a. Now think of someone you find difficult to love. Do you believe that person can change, or do you assume he or she will always be difficult to get along with? Why?

    b. Would the way you treat that person be different if you believed that he or she could grow and change? If so, how?

D And finally, love never fails. That's why love is "the greatest of these"—greater than hope or faith. Love never passes away.

15. What types of things cause love to "fail"?

16. How do you think we can develop a love that is unswayed by circumstances?

17. a. Consider the qualities of love described in 1 Corinthians 13. Indicate whether each of these qualities is true about you most of the time, some of the time, or seldom.

	True Most of the Time	True Some of the Time	Seldom True
Patient	☐	☐	☐
Kind	☐	☐	☐
Never jealous	☐	☐	☐
Not proud	☐	☐	☐
Not rude	☐	☐	☐
Doesn't insist on its own way	☐	☐	☐
Not easily angered or irritated	☐	☐	☐
Not resentful	☐	☐	☐
Slow to expose others' failings	☐	☐	☐
Hopes for the best	☐	☐	☐
Never fails	☐	☐	☐

b. In which three areas would you most like to grow? Circle them in the list above.

D If you're anything like me, after looking at this passage you will feel a bit discouraged because God has revealed some areas of life in which there's need for improvement. But let's look at verses 4-8 once more, in a different way:

> Christ in me is very patient. Christ in me is always kind. Christ in me is never jealous, never boastful. Christ in me is never arrogant or rude. Christ in me is not selfish. Christ in me is not irritable or resentful. Christ in me does not rejoice at wrong but rejoices in the right. Christ in me bears all things, believes all things, hopes all things, endures all things. Christ in me never fails.

Paul said, "Do you not realize that Christ Jesus is in you?" (2 Corinthians 13:5). That's not a figure of speech, but glorious truth! As Paul said, "Christ in you, the hope of glory" (Colossians 1:27); "I no longer live, but Christ lives in me" (Galatians 2:20).

Christ is love personified—and He lives in you. Reckon on this being true. Give the Holy Spirit the opportunity of working out these qualities in your life.

18. After discovering the importance of love in living as Jesus' follower, some believers might think they need to "work harder" at being loving. Read 1 John 4:7. According to this verse, why is this approach unlikely to be successful?

19. Read Romans 5:5 and Galatians 5:22. What is the real key to becoming more loving?

20. If this is so, how can we grow in our ability to love others? What do you think it means to "give the Holy Spirit the opportunity of working out these qualities in your life"?

21. Colossians 3:12-14 says, "As God's chosen people, holy and dearly loved, *clothe yourselves with* compassion, kindness, humility, gentleness and patience. . . . And over all these virtues *put on* love, which binds them all together in perfect unity" (emphasis added). Paul compares acting in love to putting on clothing. What does this analogy tell you about how to be loving toward others?

22. Describe the part God plays and the part we play in our becoming more loving people.

23. Think of a relationship in which you would like to become more loving. It could be with someone close to you or someone who is difficult to love. What have you learned in this study that can help you love that person the way God loves him or her?

24. Write a prayer to God, asking Him to help you become a more loving person. Pray that prayer every day for a month. You may want to enlist the help of a friend who will pray for you.

Parting Thought

"This is how we know what love is: Jesus laid down his life for us" (1 John 3:16). *No explanation of love's meaning is easier to understand than this statement of what Jesus did for those He loved—He gave Himself. As His followers, we are to do the same thing. It is in the giving of ourselves that we love.*

—Tom Jones, "Love in Other Words," Issue 79

3

Putting Others First

Love is probably the most important element in building godly relationships. But running a close second to love is humility—that is, considering others' feelings, desires, and rights to be as important as—or even more important than—our own. Look at any offense or conflict in your life, and you'll likely find pride lurking in the wings—an insistence on having your own way, an attitude that you are more important than others.

1. Has pride damaged your relationships in the past? Check any of the following that are true.

   ☐ I can get so focused on my agenda that I run over people.
   ☐ I sometimes think of myself as better than others.
   ☐ I have difficulty apologizing when I've done something wrong.
   ☐ I pass up opportunities to serve—at home, at work, or at church—because it would take up too much of my time.
   ☐ I'm sometimes more interested in talking than in listening and asking questions.
   ☐ I don't want to associate with believers who keep struggling with sin.
   ☐ I expect other people to take the initiative in friendships.
   ☐ I find it difficult to receive negative feedback.
   ☐ Other (describe):

Humility, on the other hand, tears down walls and builds bridges by communicating to others how important they are to us.

Christlike relationships require us to humble ourselves, to lay down our lives for others.

2.   Think of a person you know who is humble. How do you see that humility lived out in his or her relationships?

In this portion of the article entitled "**Haughty or Humble?**" **by Howard Baker** (excerpted from Issue 105), the author offers several questions we can ask ourselves to test the level of humility in our relationships.

Am I a Servant of All?

After a display of pride by some of His disciples, Jesus reminded them, "Whoever wants to become great among you must be your servant, and whoever wants to be first must be slave of all" (Mark 10:43-44; see verses 35-45).

In *Celebration of Discipline*, Richard Foster wisely makes the distinction between "choosing to serve and choosing to be a servant." Choosing to serve allows me to stay comfortably in charge. I decide when, where, and whom I will serve. This kind of service can actually produce pride rather than humility, as the focus remains on what is good for me. On the other hand, when I choose to be a servant, I have placed myself "on call" to the needs of others.

In Mark 10:51 Jesus demonstrates the humble demeanor of a servant when He asks blind Bartimaeus, "What do you want me to do for you?" Unlike Jesus, I frequently presume to know what people need and base my serving on the agenda I set for them. I may think I am serving my wife by doing household chores when what she really needs is relaxed conversation over a cup of coffee. "How can I help you?" is the constant question of the humble servant. Imagine the impact this simple question would have on our children, our employers, our neighbors, and our friends. They may even begin to see Jesus, as Bartimaeus did.

3. Mark 10:45 says that Jesus "did not come to be served, but to serve." After some honest reflection, mark an X at the place on the spectrum that best reflects your attitude.

- At work:

|———————————————————————————————————|
Want to be served   Want to serve

- At home:

|———————————————————————————————————|
Want to be served   Want to serve

- At church:

|———————————————————————————————————|
Want to be served   Want to serve

4. In which arena—work, home, or church—do you find it most natural to want to serve? Why?

5. Choose the area in question three in which you most often find yourself wanting to *be* served. In that arena, what would it look like in the following week to . . .

- Choose to serve?

- Choose to be a servant?

6. Choose three people you know and ask them in the coming week, "How can I best help you?" Record their answers below.

Name   How I Can Best Help

Do I Associate with the Lowly?

"Do not be proud," Paul wrote, "but be willing to associate with people of low position. Do not be conceited" (Romans 12:16).

James flatly stated that if you show partiality, you are committing sin (see James 2:1-9). In that situation the partiality was based on the appearance of wealth. One person came to church dressed in fine clothes and jewelry and was given a seat of honor. A poor person came in and was told to stand in the back. James said that showing this kind of personal favoritism arises out of evil motives.

Both personally and corporately we must examine our motives and practices in this regard if we are serious about being clothed in humility toward one another.

Jesus' humility led Him to become the "friend of tax collectors and 'sinners'" (Luke 5:30), as well as prostitutes, thieves, and other outcasts. The glance and stance of Jesus was always toward the poor and the powerless. He practiced downward mobility. He gravitated toward those who desperately needed Him. In light of Jesus' example, we must ask ourselves, "Who are my friends?"

The Colorado Prayer Luncheon is an event that attracts the wealthy, powerful, and famous in our community. A friend of mine had been given an extra ticket, and he asked a street person to attend with him. My friend thought it would be fitting to invite someone who needed a good meal. He chose to associate with the lowly. I thought to myself, *That is what Jesus would have done.*

7. The following types of people are often dismissed by our society—and even within our churches. How easy do you find it to associate with people in each of these groups? Circle the appropriate numbers.

	Easy				Difficult
Poorly dressed	1	2	3	4	5
Children	1	2	3	4	5
Another race	1	2	3	4	5
Teenagers	1	2	3	4	5
Mentally handicapped	1	2	3	4	5
Uneducated	1	2	3	4	5
Elderly	1	2	3	4	5
Single	1	2	3	4	5

8. a. Tell about a time when you reached out to someone of "low position."

b. Did the experience change you? If so, how?

D Do I Consider Others More Important than Myself?

Paul wrote, "Do nothing out of selfish ambition or vain conceit, but in humility consider others better than yourselves" (Philippians 2:3). A self-centered life is not a Christian life. Yet the subtleties of pride creep in disguised as angels of light. I am told to be goal-oriented so I can be "highly effective." I am encouraged to be "significant" for God. The fallacy in all of the "doing" is that I, rather than Christ, become the center. How can I consider others more important than myself when I have so much to do to get my act together? I can't.

That's why trust in God's provision is key to learning this aspect of humility. If He will meet all my needs, including my need to be transformed into His likeness, then I can focus less on doing and more on being, less on myself and more on others.

There was a young man with cerebral palsy who incarnated this truth to me. I was on the staff of a Young Life camp in the mountains of Colorado, and Steve was on the work crew. The rugged terrain made it very difficult for him to get around, yet I never heard him complain, and he always greeted me with a smile. One of our staff had been troubled by a toothache and made no secret of it for several days. After he returned from the dentist, Steve approached him with sincere concern and compassion and inquired about the tooth. The staff member was stopped in his tracks. He realized that a minor toothache had caused him to be totally self-centered. In contrast, Steve had entrusted his lifelong debilitating illness to God, leaving him free to demonstrate true concern for others.

When I trust my loving Father to care for my needs, I am free to consider others more important than myself.

9. The author says that being preoccupied with getting our needs met can cause us to focus on ourselves instead of others. Which of the following tend to occupy your thoughts and energy? Check all that apply.

☐ Issues with my job
☐ My hobbies/interests
☐ My family
☐ Projects around the home
☐ My finances
☐ My personal ministry
☐ My health
☐ My friendships
☐ My desire to be married
☐ Hurts that I struggle to forgive

☐ Future goals

☐ Other (describe):

10. a. When you spend time with others, are you more inclined to talk about your needs and interests or the other person's? Mark an X at the place on the spectrum that best reflects your conversations.

├───┤
Tend to talk   Tend to listen
about myself   to others

b. Would a spiritually mature person's X be in the middle or at the far right? Explain your answer.

11. How could learning to trust God to meet your needs free you to focus more on others?

12. Think of a time in the next week when you will get together with someone close to you, such as spending time with a friend or talking to your spouse or roommate after work. What are three questions you could ask that person to show your interest in him or her?

■

■

■

Am I Willing to Take the Lower Place?

In the parable found in Luke 14:7-11, the dinner guests are vying for the best places at the table. The conclusion of the parable in Jesus' words is, "For everyone who exalts himself will be humbled, and he who humbles himself will be exalted." Peter, in his first letter, adds that God will exalt the humble "in due time" (1 Peter 5:6). This is what makes taking the lower place so challenging. It may be a long time before I am asked to move up.

This story about Senator Mark Hatfield, who powerfully displayed Christ in the world of politics, encourages me to take the lower place. He attended a weekly Bible study luncheon at his church in Washington along with many other politicians and professionals. When the meeting was over, most people would rush back to their important business. Senator Hatfield, however, could often be seen folding and stacking chairs after everyone else had left. No one in attendance had the magnitude of responsibilities that he had. Nevertheless, he chose to stay, to take the lower place of doing the menial task, much as Jesus did by taking the towel and the basin at the Last Supper and washing the disciples' feet. When Jesus had finished, He called us all to the lower place: "I have set you an example that you should do as I have done for you" (John 13:15).

13. Read Luke 14:7-11. What are some ways in which believers today have the opportunity to "take the lower place"? (Think of the home, the workplace, church, and other day-to-day situations, such as traffic and grocery store lines.)

How Do I Respond to Criticism?

The acid test of my humility is how I respond when I am criticized, opposed, or persecuted.

Jesus said that we are to love our enemies and pray for those who persecute us (Matthew 5:44). Paul added, "Do not repay anyone evil for evil" (Romans 12:17). Do I pray for those who criticize me? Am I an agent of Christ's love to those with whom I disagree? Or do I take the easy path and love only those who love me? Jesus prayed for forgiveness for those who crucified Him, and we are called to follow in His steps.

14. Read 2 Samuel 16:5-14, focusing especially on verse 9.

   a. How did Abishai want to respond to Shimei's attack on David?

   b. What was David's response?

   Now focus on verses 10-12 and respond to the following question.

   c. How did his response display humility?

15. Think of the last time you were criticized. If David had been in your shoes, how might he have responded?

D Is Humility Possible?

A life of humility toward others seems beyond my reach. How could I ever live at that level?

If the acid test of our humility is our relationships, then Jesus is our perfect model. Our pride is overcome, vanquished, when our focus and our energy are directed to becoming less like us and more like the One who is gentle and humble in heart.

16. Think again about how pride and humility affect the way you treat people. Complete the following sentences, listing several ideas under each one.

    ▪ When I am proud, I . . .
    (*For example, ". . . think only about my own objectives."*)

    ▪ When I am humble, I . . .
    (*For example, ". . . take time to serve others when there's nothing in it for me."*)

17. What ideas or Scriptures from this study stood out to you the most?

18. How do you sense God is asking you to respond to what you've learned?

4

Caring for Christians

What is fellowship? Is it merely Christians getting together, or is it something more? How can you tell if true fellowship has taken place?

1.   How would you define fellowship?

In the following article entitled "**Steps to Biblical Fellowship**" **by Jerry Bridges** (excerpted from Issue 36), the author explores the kinds of relationships that God intends for believers, and he shows us how to pursue them.

Better than One

I believe Christians have largely overlooked their responsibility to mutually care for one another. The Scriptures command us to instruct, teach, admonish, encourage, stimulate, and build up one another. We are to pray for one another and carry one another's burdens. We are to allow others to have a caring ministry in our own lives. Still another group of Scriptures sets forth our responsibility to help one another physically and materially.

   One Old Testament passage has helped me organize my thoughts into four areas of responsibility in caring for others. Ecclesiastes 4:9-12 begins with the statement, "Two are better than one," followed by four reasons why that is true. These four reasons are the four mental pegs upon which I hang my responsibility to care for others and to allow others to care for me:

> Two are better than one, because they have a good return for their work: If one falls down, his friend can help him up. . . . Also, if two lie down together, they will keep warm. But how can one keep warm alone? Though one may be overpowered, two can defend themselves. A cord of three strands is not quickly broken.

Sharpening One Another

The first reason that two are better than one is "because they have a good return for their work" (verse 9). In almost any endeavor, whether it's cleaning out the garage or doing Bible study, two people working together can produce more results than the total of their efforts working alone. In science, this is called synergism. A friend of mine describes the synergistic effect as "one plus one equals three."

The principle of synergism applies even more in the area of Christian growth in understanding and applying the Scriptures to our lives. We are to teach and admonish one another and instruct one another (Romans 15:14; Colossians 3:16). As Solomon puts it elsewhere, we are to sharpen one another "as iron sharpens iron" (Proverbs 27:17). And when we find ourselves on the receiving end of such teaching, admonishment, or sharpening we are to submit to one another (Ephesians 5:21).

All of us, at various times, need someone to sharpen us, to help us understand the Scriptures more accurately or apply them better, or to keep us from getting off balance on some truth. But this is delicate work. Though we all need this sharpening, we all resist it because of our fragile self-esteem. Therefore, sharpening must be mutual and must be done within an atmosphere of caring for one another.

Most of us are familiar with the concept of "speaking the truth in love" (Ephesians 4:15). It is usually applied in a subjective way—that is, of loving confrontation about a need in another person's life. But the context indicates it is the truth of Scripture that Paul had in view. We are to speak the truth of Scripture, sharpening one another in love, so that we may grow together.

2.   How have you seen two or more people working together produce much more than they could have produced individually?

3.   Describe a time when you benefited from the "sharpening" of another believer.

4.   In Acts 18:24-26, we find the story of Apollos, a godly man who needed to be sharpened.

   a. When Priscilla and Aquila perceived that he needed help, what did they do?

   b. How did their approach show that they cared for him?

5.   Why is it important to take a loving approach to someone who needs sharpening?

6. After David committed adultery and arranged for the death of his lover's husband, God sent Nathan the prophet to confront him (2 Samuel 12:1-13). What approach did Nathan take?

7. According to verse 13, how did David respond to Nathan?

8. What can you learn from Nathan about effective "sharpening"?

9. Galatians 6:1 gives us two principles for correcting someone who is caught in sin. What are they?

   ▪

   ▪

10. Galatians 6:2 says, "Carry each other's burdens, and in this way you will fulfill the law of Christ." How does this idea tie in with correcting someone who is sinning?

Encouraging One Another

The second reason two are better than one is, "If one falls down, his friend can help him up" (Ecclesiastes 4:10). This passage speaks to me of encouragement, one of the greatest needs in the body of Christ today. Of the ten passages I have found that speak about caring for one another, four of them tell us to encourage one another: 1 Thessalonians 4:18 and 5:11; Hebrews 3:13 and 10:25.

To encourage is to inspire another with courage. Courage is the mental or spiritual strength to persevere in the face of difficulty. So to encourage someone is to fortify that person with the spiritual strength to persevere in spite of hardship. The Greek word translated as "encourage" in the New Testament communicates the idea of one person standing alongside another giving appropriate counsel.

The writer of Hebrews, who twice tells us to encourage one another, beautifully illustrates his instructions with his own example. He tells his readers, "So do not throw away your confidence; it will be richly rewarded. You need to persevere so that when you have done the will of God, you will receive what he has promised" (Hebrews 10:35-36). His readers were facing severe pressure to turn from their faith. Many of them were suffering persecution, some had been thrown into prison, and others had had their property confiscated. They needed encouragement from him, but they also needed to encourage one another.

The body of Christ needs encouragers today. Most of us in the Western world are not facing the severe trials that the Hebrew Christians faced, but many in the body are discouraged because of other conflicts. Some face marital difficulties, others have heartaches over rebellious or spiritually indifferent children. Some face demotion or even loss of their jobs. Many are wondering if God truly cares for them, and they certainly don't believe that any other person cares.

So we need to learn to encourage one another. We must not depend solely on our pastors or other spiritual leaders to do this. We must also do it ourselves. But we must remember that to encourage is to fortify one another with the strength to endure. It does not mean to commiserate with one another over our respective trials and difficulties. As Paul said elsewhere, we are to speak only what is helpful for building others up, according to their needs

(Ephesians 4:29). So as we care for one another, we must demonstrate care and compassion, but not pity. The other person must know we care, but more importantly, he or she must know that God cares. That is the objective of encouragement.

11. As you read the preceding paragraphs, did any people who need encouragement come to mind? If so, write their names below.

12. God sent an encourager to the apostle Paul, someone who helped in his ministry and stood by him when he was imprisoned. In 2 Timothy 1:16-18, Paul cites four ways in which Onesiphorus encouraged him. Think of someone you know who needs encouragement. How could you follow Onesiphorus's example in that person's life?

What Onesiphorus Did	What You Could Do
"He often refreshed me."	
"He . . . was not ashamed of my chains."	
"He searched hard for me until he found me."	
"In . . . many ways he helped me in Ephesus."	

13. a. What do you think is the difference between showing compassion and showing pity?

   b. What is the effect of each of these on the hurting person's life?

14. We want our words to build others up (Ephesians 4:29), but how can we know that what we say will be helpful? One way is to remind them of the uplifting truths in God's Word.

   a. Choose one of the people you listed in question eleven and write his or her name in the margin. Which of the following Scriptures might most encourage this person? Place a check mark beside it.

   ☐ Jeremiah 32:27—"I am the LORD, the God of all mankind. Is anything too hard for me?"
   ☐ Isaiah 41:10—"Do not fear, for I am with you; do not be dismayed, for I am your God. I will strengthen you and help you; I will uphold you with my righteous right hand."
   ☐ Matthew 11:28-30—"Come to me, all you who are weary and burdened, and I will give you rest. Take my yoke upon you and learn from me, for I am gentle and humble in heart, and you will find rest for your souls. For my yoke is easy and my burden is light."
   ☐ Romans 8:38—"I am convinced that neither death nor life, neither angels nor demons, neither the present nor the future, nor any powers, neither height nor depth, nor anything else in all creation, will be able to separate us from the love of God that is in Christ Jesus our Lord."
   ☐ Other (write one of your favorite Scriptures here):

b. How might you share that Scripture with the person you chose? Set aside a time to do it this week.

15. In her article "Practical Encouragement" (Issue 113), Jeanne Zornes describes the following eight "encouragement styles." Which of them sounds most like you? In other words, which do you most enjoy and find yourself effective at doing? Check one or more.

  ☐ Speaking
  ☐ Writing
  ☐ Being with someone
  ☐ Touching
  ☐ Praying
  ☐ Showing hospitality
  ☐ Giving
  ☐ Helping

16. How could you use your encouragement style this week to lift up someone who needs it?

D Stimulating One Another

The third reason two are better than one is that together "they will keep warm" (Ecclesiastes 4:11). This speaks of stimulating one another, or to use the words of Hebrews 10:24, to "spur one another on toward love and good deeds." We are prone not only to discouragement but also to lethargy. We get tired of fulfilling our responsibilities in the body. We are all prone to live for ourselves rather than others, so we need to be spurred on.

One of my friends used to refer to the mutual stimulus of a small band of men and women ministering together as the "warmth of the pack." My favorite illustration of this principle is the charcoal briquettes in a backyard grill. When you want to get the charcoal hot enough to cook meat, you pile all the briquettes together. If one briquette is removed from the pile, it quickly loses its heat. We are much like the charcoal briquettes. Left to ourselves, our zeal for Christian service quickly dissipates. We need to be constantly stimulated.

Note how the writer of Hebrews again illustrates his teaching by his own example. In chapter 13, he spurs his readers on with such exhortations as, "Do not forget to entertain strangers. . . . Remember those in prison. . . . Do not forget to do good and to share with others" (Hebrews 13:2,3,16).

Think what obedience to this instruction could mean in our churches and other Christian ministries! What if, instead of a pastor always having to exhort his flock, the flock was always exhorting one another? Think what might happen if we urged one another to be more active in evangelism or to give more to missions. Or if the students in a campus ministry took the initiative to stimulate each other to doing deeds of kindness. But this is exactly what we are supposed to do. We are to stimulate one another.

17.	What kinds of stimulation are most motivating for you? Check one or more.

☐ Having someone share Scripture with me
☐ Seeing someone else's example
☐ Being challenged by a teacher or pastor in a group setting
☐ Being challenged one-on-one
☐ Hearing about someone else's experience
☐ Reading a book or article
☐ Other (describe):

18. a. Think of a believer or group of believers you feel close to—
your family, your small group, or longtime friends. In which of
the areas below do you think they most need "spurring on"?

☐ Remembering that God is in control of their circumstances
☐ Being faithful to spend time in God's Word
☐ Sharing the gospel with unbelievers
☐ Caring for the poor
☐ Using their spiritual gifts to serve others
☐ Putting the kingdom of God first in their life
☐ Demonstrating character qualities such as love, humility,
and honesty
☐ Other (describe):

b. Choose one of the areas you marked above and write it on
the line below. What are three ways in which you might
stimulate someone to be faithful in this area?

_____

■

■

■

Defending One Another

The fourth reason two are better than one is that "though one may
be overpowered, two can defend themselves" (Ecclesiastes 4:12).
I believe it was Martin Luther who first coined the phrase, "the
world, the flesh, and the devil." We are all subject to attack from all
three of these enemies, and we need each other to defend ourselves.
That is why James said to "confess your sins to each other and pray
for each other so that you may be healed" (James 5:16).

Of the four aspects of spiritual care for one another, this one is probably the most difficult. We are afraid to be vulnerable enough to allow someone else to see our struggles and temptations, let alone our sins and failures. We need to realize, however, that Scripture calls for a mutual relationship, a mutual openness and praying for one another. If I expect to help someone else defend himself against temptation or the attacks of Satan, I must be willing to allow him to help me.

How do we help each other defend ourselves against temptation or Satan's attacks? James 5:16 gives us two necessary weapons: openness with one another and prayer. A third important weapon is accountability to one another. Accountability in a "mutual defense pact" is simply an agreement to allow others to check up on us. Suppose I am having difficulty getting up in the morning to have my quiet time. I might allow you to ask me how I am doing regularly, or I might even ask you to call me every day at 6 A.M. to see if I am up and going.

Openness, accountability, and prayer must all have equal weight in our defense of each other. Openness alone will eventually result in an ungodly acceptance of the status quo. We may become comfortable sharing our sins and failures and lose any motivation to change. Accountability without prayer results in legalism, seeking to please another person. There is also the danger of exerting a spiritual authoritarianism over those who have become accountable to us if we are not wrestling in prayer on their behalf. Prayer without openness fails to deal with the real issues in each other's lives. Prayer without accountability fails to recognize both the divine and the human element in spiritual warfare. Nehemiah, when faced with the probability of an enemy attack, "prayed to . . . God and posted a guard day and night to meet this threat" (Nehemiah 4:9). Having accountability is "posting a guard." We need prayer and we need to post the guard.

19. a. Which of the three defenses seems most difficult to make a part of your life? Check one.

☐ Openness
☐ Accountability
☐ Prayer

b. Why is the area you checked so difficult?

c. What might help you overcome this difficulty? (If you're not sure, talk to another believer who seems to be strong in this area.)

20. Is there an area of your life in which you need the protection provided by openness, accountability, and prayer? What is it?

21. How could you begin to take advantage of the help available in this kind of relationship?

22. Are you willing to offer mutual openness, accountability, and prayer to another believer who needs protection against the Enemy? What would be the next step toward pursuing or growing in such a relationship?

Taking the Initiative

It is important to realize that none of these four ways of caring for one another requires a crisis situation. Rather, we are to care for one another on a daily basis. Quite possibly, such daily caring would avert a lot of crisis situations in the body.

Neither are these four ways of caring a reactive ministry—waiting until others come to us for help, or until their needs for care become obvious. Rather, we are to take the initiative to care for one another. This means we need to develop a spiritual "radar" that is constantly scanning to locate those who need spiritual care. It means we must take a genuine interest in the welfare of others, as well as looking out for our own interests (Philippians 2:20-21).

23. a. Which of the four areas from Ecclesiastes 4 is strongest in your relationships with other believers? Put a star by it. Which one needs the most growth in your life? Put a check mark next to it.

__ Sharpening

__ Encouraging

__ Stimulating

__ Defending

b. What is one thing you could do this week to practice the area in which you're strongest?

c. What is one thing you could do to develop the area that most needs growth?

24. What one idea do you most want to take away from this study?

5

Building Close Friendships

Most of us have friends. But how many of us have intimate friend-ships—the kind where we are free to be who we are? Are our relationships deep enough to have significant spiritual impact on our lives?

In the following article entitled **"Closer than a Brother" by Paul Thigpen** (excerpted from Issue 54), the author talks about how we can build the kind of friendships that satisfy our souls and help us grow closer to Jesus. He shares his insights from Scripture as well as from his friendships with two men, Lee and Dave.

 The Treasure of Intimacy

The petals of the roses I'd gathered for my daughter lay scattered around the vase that still held their naked stems. Lydia, my six-year-old, was pointing to them and weeping uncontrollably.

I knew that our impending move to another city had left her emotionally fragile, so I took Lydia in my arms and offered words of comfort: "Sweetheart, that's just how roses are. We get to enjoy them a day or two, and then the petals fall."

But Lydia blurted out a protest through the sobs: "The petals didn't fall off. I *tore* them off! I pretended those roses were my heart, and my heart is torn all to pieces because I'm leaving my friends."

Then the two of us wept in one another's arms. In perfect con-crete poetry, Lydia had described the condition of both our hearts. Over several years we had each cultivated a pair of intimate friend-ships. To have such friends torn from us was truly to have our hearts torn apart, and to realize the value of the relationships that had grown.

Ⓓ Places in the Heart

My relationships with Dave and Lee are distinguished by a rare depth and breadth. I've concluded that the precious quality that is making my separation from these friends so costly is the shared treasure of *intimacy*.

What exactly do we mean when we speak of an "intimate" friendship? "There is a friend," says the book of Proverbs, "who sticks *closer* than a brother" (18:24, emphasis added)—a friend who, we might say, even goes beyond "close" all the way to "inside." The Latin root of our word *intimacy* is actually the superlative of *intus*, "within." So the friend who is intimate is literally the one who is "most within" us, the one we have taken into the deepest chamber of our heart, into the most inward, private, and vulnerable place we have.

Scripture provides us with evidence of intimate friendships. In my own cries of grief I hear echoes of godly men in Scripture weeping over their separation from each other. David and Jonathan "kissed each other and wept together" when national politics sent David fleeing for his life (1 Samuel 20:41). The apostle Paul and the Ephesian elders wept, embraced, and kissed on the beach as Paul departed for Jerusalem (Acts 20:36-38). And in what is perhaps the Bible's most poignant scene of separated friends, Jesus gazed on the tomb of His beloved Lazarus and wept (John 11:35).

I believe that all these men were paying the price of genuine intimacy with godly friends who had found their way deep into their hearts. And I believe that they all paid the price gladly for the sake of a treasure that transformed their lives by drawing them deep into the heart of God as well.

1. How do you react when you hear the phrase "intimate friendship"? Check one.

    ☐ Grateful: I have a few intimate friendships that enrich my life.
    ☐ Skeptical: It's something I desire, but I wonder if it's really possible in this world.
    ☐ Threatened: How could anyone who knew me inside and out still love me?

☐ Indifferent: I get along pretty well on my own—I don't need that kind of relationship.

☐ Intrigued: I long for that kind of closeness with a few others.

☐ Guarded: I let someone get that close once, and I got burned. Never again.

☐ Other (describe):

2. The story of David and Jonathan gives us one of the best pictures of intimate friendship found in Scripture. Read 1 Samuel 20, then record the evidences of the deep friendship you find.

■ Verses 5-7,24-31

■ Verse 9

■ Verses 16,42

■ Verse 17

■ Verse 32

■ Verse 34

3. What signs of their close friendship do you see even after Jonathan dies in battle?

■ 2 Samuel 1:17-27

■ 2 Samuel 9

4. What do you find most attractive about David and Jonathan's friendship?

D The Divine Pattern

We can discover the perfect model of intimacy in the heart of God. There, in an eternally intimate relationship, the Father and the Son are "most within" each other: "I am in the Father," said Jesus, "and the Father is in me" (John 14:11).

Jesus said, "Just as the Father knows me [so] I know the Father" (John 10:15). Jesus *knew* the Father—knew His character, His thoughts, His heart, His will. Jesus was able to minister in grace and power because from moment to moment He knew what the Father was doing and acted accordingly (John 5:19). And the Father knew the Son just as deeply and completely. This kind of knowing extends to those who enter into life in Christ: "I know my sheep," Jesus said, "and my sheep know me" (John 10:14).

Deep mutual knowledge, I believe, is the practical content of the term *intimacy*. Intimate friends have opened the doors of who they are and invited the other to come in. They may begin with short visits into the "living rooms" of each other's hearts, but intimacy grows as they allow each other to come further and further inside. The intimate friend has seen within me both the fancy furniture and the dirty laundry, the carefully made beds and the dust balls under them.

The Details and the Depths

My intimacy with Lee and Dave reflects this kind of familiarity. I know the details about Lee and Dave that most others never notice. If Lee comes up from behind me, I immediately recognize his cologne; if it's Dave, I recognize the smell of the fabric softener on his clothes.

I know Lee and Dave's temperaments: Lee is a questioner, Dave is a teaser. Dave responds first and reflects later; Lee reverses the process.

I know that Dave focuses on tasks but Lee focuses on thoughts. Dave, for example, gives himself permission to spend time with people when he can do something practical for them. So to get him over to my home for fellowship, I may ask him to help repair my kitchen linoleum. On the other hand, Lee and I are better off spending time together without a task. The intensity of our conversation often preempts our labor.

As friends we've gone even deeper than personality traits in the process of our mutual discovery. Over time, as we've learned to trust each other, we've slowly opened up to each other the broken and needy places inside as well, knowing that we will not be rejected.

We know each other's painful pasts, our current struggles, our apprehensions about the future. I know Lee's fears of inadequacy in his vocation, and Dave's fears of inadequacy as a father. They know my fears in both regards.

In all these ways and countless more, I know Lee and Dave, and I am known by them. As Christian brothers, we share an intimacy that reflects dimly, yet accurately, the intimacy we have with God.

5. Psalm 139 shows us several aspects of intimacy with God. In the left column, write what you learn from each passage about a close relationship with God. In the right column, reflect on how that kind of intimacy could be experienced in human friendships.

Intimacy with God	Human Friendships
▪ Verses 1-4	
▪ Verses 7-10	
▪ Verses 11-12	
▪ Verse 17	

6. a. In what ways is intimacy with God similar to intimacy with people?

b. In what ways is it different?

7. a. How well do you know your closest same-sex friend, and how well does he or she know you? Use a "Y" for yes, an "N" for no, and a "?" if you're not sure.

	I know this about my friend	My friend knows this about me
Favorite type of music		
Favorite hobbies		
Ideal vacation		
Job		
Feelings about job		
What growing-up years were like		
Quality of marriage or feelings about singleness		
Relationship with kids		
Greatest fears		
Persistent struggles		
Spiritual gifts		
Greatest strengths		

b. Choose one area in which you'd like to learn more about your friend and write it on the line below. Also, write three questions you could ask that friend the next time you get together.

_____

-

-

-

Dirty Laundry

A thorough knowledge of who I am includes much in my heart that is unpleasant or even frightening. As the psalmist noted, intimacy with God means that God discovers the darkness and the sinfulness within (Psalm 139:12,23-24). Yet God has chosen to love me despite the dirty laundry and the dust balls. He has willingly taken up residence inside me as I am.

No wonder, then, that intimacy with God is the best foundation for intimacy with Christian friends. Once we've allowed God inside our deepest chambers and discovered that He can love us enough to remain there despite what He finds, we have the courage to hope that someone else could know and love us that way. We realize as well that the risk, and even the pain, is worth it all for the sake of having a friend settle down "inside us."

8. Paul wrote in Romans 8:35,38-39, "Who shall separate us from the love of Christ? . . . I am convinced that neither death nor life, neither angels nor demons, neither the present nor

the future, nor any powers, neither height nor depth, nor anything else in all creation, will be able to separate us from the love of God that is in Christ Jesus our Lord." When we develop intimate friendships, we risk being rejected and hurt. How can experiencing intimacy with God give us the courage to take the risk?

Building Intimacy

The home that is our heart remains a lonely place without at least one or two intimate friends to live there with us. Of course, we can't invite everyone in to stay; that would make our home a hotel. Even Jesus asked only three of the Twelve to share in vulnerable moments such as His agonized prayer in Gethsemane (Mark 14:32-41). But by God's grace we can find a few friends who are willing to know us thoroughly and yet love us faithfully. How is such a dwelling place constructed?

Common Faith. First, the only sure foundation for intimacy between Christian friends is a faith in God that allows us to risk trusting others. A firm conviction that it's possible for Someone both to know us truly and to love us unconditionally provides secure ground on which to build.

Common Interests. Second, we need a defined area of our hearts in which we can grow familiar with each other. Shared values and experiences provide "walls"—boundaries that mark what belongs to us in common.

I share with both Dave and Lee, for example, a love for making music. So some of the richest moments I've had with each of them—moments which have taken us deeper into each other—were times when we ministered together musically.

Time Together. Building the walls of intimacy takes time. My friendships with Lee and Dave have tended to deepen in proportion to the amount of time we spend together. Sometimes we labor together, serving in the church or working on a car. Other times we simply schedule time to picnic in a park or escape to the mountains for a weekend. To become intimate, we need a growing pool of shared experiences.

Evidently Jesus realized this principle of intimate friendship in His intentional use of time with Peter, James, and John. On several occasions He took them aside to spend time with Him, sharing a significant experience such as the raising of a young girl (Luke 8:51-55) or the Transfiguration on the mountain (Matthew 17:1-2). After they had been with Jesus on those occasions, we shouldn't be surprised that He was willing to allow them entrance into the moment of His deepest grief in the garden.

Vulnerability. Even so, time together is not enough to ensure intimacy. A fourth element of the process—the doorways we build into the home of our heart—includes those intentional acts of self-disclosure in which we risk revealing who we are.

One evening I cried on Dave's shoulder for what seemed like an eternity, telling him about the deepest areas of brokenness in my life. The door I opened into my heart that night gave him entrance into other inner rooms, places where he could sit down and say, "Even in this untidy place, I intend to settle in and help you clean up." Meanwhile, he opened up to me as well, and I found the courage to love him as he had loved me.

Sensitivity. A home without windows would be dark and blind. So we need places to look outside ourselves, to turn our attention toward the friend at our door. Intimacy requires more than opening ourselves; we must also look to our friend, forgetting ourselves and cultivating a sensitivity to the other's heart. If I'm struggling, Lee and Dave know it, even when other friends don't. They've made themselves sensitive to the clues I give about my thoughts and feelings, and they respond according to my needs.

Loyalty. Sixth, loyalty is the roof that covers an intimate friendship with protection. Dave and I have on occasion irritated each other; Lee and I have disagreed. But through it all our loyalty to each other has more than kept our friendship intact; it has deepened our intimacy. Ruth's attitude toward Naomi has become our own: Even if one of us should tell the other to go away, the other would refuse to leave (Ruth 1:16-18).

Prayer. Finally, prayer is the hearth of the home where my intimate friends have come to dwell. In earlier generations, the hearth not only heated a house, it was the place where nourishment was prepared. In a similar way, prayer warms and feeds our friendship as nothing else can. Just as Jesus knew the weakness of His intimate friend Peter and prayed for him (Luke 22:31-32), we're able to pray knowledgeably and effectively for each other as no one else can.

9. What differences have you noticed between your friendships with fellow believers and your friendships with unbelievers?

10. Choose two or three of your closest friends and write their names below. Then, after each name, list the interests you share with these people.

    ■

    ■

    ■

11. a. How could you find more quality time to spend with friends? List some specific ideas below for activities you could do together (such as exercise, projects, ministry, hobbies).

    b. Choose a friend you'd like to grow closer to. Then pick one or two of these ideas to implement. Schedule some time together in the next two weeks.

c. Which of these activities could you do with someone on a regular basis, such as weekly or biweekly? Consider scheduling a standing "date" for spending time together with at least one friend.

12. Matthew tells us that in the Garden of Gethsemane, Jesus chose Peter, James, and John to be with Him in His time of distress. Read Matthew 26:36-38. How did Jesus display vulnerability to His friends?

13. Mark on the line below the true nature of your heart when you share with your close friends. Do you find it easy to "spill your guts," or do you find it difficult to go beyond sharing facts to sharing feelings with others?

_____

Very vulnerable   Very guarded

14. If you need to grow in vulnerability, what would be the next step for you?

15. Describe a time when a close friend showed sensitivity to you, and how that affected your friendship.

16. Describe a time when a close friend showed loyalty to you, and how that affected your friendship.

17. a. How has prayer deepened your friendships in the past?

   b. How might you make prayer a more integral part of your friendships now? List three specific ideas.

   ■

   ■

   ■

D Power to Transform

Our trusting friendship with God allows us room to trust a friend; our intimacy with God makes possible our intimacy with others. At the same time, the beauty of an intimate friendship with another Christian is its power to complete the circle. The more deeply I establish a mutual residence in the heart of a friend, the more deeply I find myself able to abide in Christ.

   My intimate friendships with Lee and Dave have played a role in God's strategy to renew His own image in me (Colossians 3:10). Lee and Dave have reflected back to me their knowledge of me in ways that correct and clarify my self-understanding, adding new honesty to my walk with God. My knowledge of them has broadened and deepened my appreciation of human nature and of God's nature as well.

In their loving acceptance I've found the courage to forgive myself and to change. In their strengths my weaknesses have found compensation. The incomplete pieces of who I am are being joined into a new wholeness that includes who they are, a knitting together of souls like David and Jonathan knew (see 1 Samuel 18:1, NASB). And no matter how far apart we may live, that abiding wholeness is a sign that we have found in each other's heart a permanent residence.

Meanwhile, the oneness of faith and love that I share with Dave and Lee brightens my hope in the Lord. As a delightful foretaste of the ultimate intimacy we'll share in Christ at the consummation of all things, intimate friendship is like marriage in that it provides us with a picture of deeper, more beautiful realities that await us in God (Ephesians 5:32).

With that in mind, I plan to have a talk with my daughter, Lydia, again someday about the price and the promise of intimacy. Despite the pain of separation, I can offer firm words of hope: These petals may fall, my darling, but the roots will only run deeper, and the rose will bloom again to live forever.

18.   Think of your relationships with your closest Christian friends. How have these friends . . .

   ▪ Helped you understand God's love for and acceptance of you?

   ▪ Challenged you to become more Christlike?

   ▪ Compensated for your weaknesses?

19. How would your life be different today if you had never had close Christian friends?

20. Look back over the article and your answers to the questions. Is there anything you would like to do to deepen, preserve, or renew one or more close friendships? What is it?

Parting Thought

Friendships are best maintained in the midst of the spiritual battle. . . . A working partnership in a common spiritual endeavor, whether encouraging each other to grow in discipleship or reaching out to others in evangelism, will build a deeper foundation than a relationship centered simply on spending time together and talking.

—Jerry and Mary White, "The Strength of Friendship," Issue 11

6

Learning to Forgive

If we are involved with people, sooner or later we will need to forgive.

Some of us have suffered offenses that led to excruciating loss: abuse by a parent, adultery or abandonment by a spouse, a child's murder, betrayal by a friend. The rest of us struggle with wounds that, though not as catastrophic, can still eat us alive with each remembrance or each new slight. Even the smallest offense can lead to bitterness that robs us of fellowship with God and joy in living.

For the follower of Jesus, forgiving everyone who hurts us is not an option; it is a duty. Yet it is one of the most difficult things that our Lord asks us to do.

In the following article entitled "**Free to Forgive**" **by Kathy E. Dahlen** (excerpted from Issue 105), the author describes what forgiveness is and how we can find the power to let go of the past.

What Forgiveness Is Not

We can begin to understand forgiveness by looking at what it is not.

Forgiveness is not a cover-up or a game of "let's pretend." It is not a performance in which we shrug our shoulders and pretend the offense was "no big deal."

Forgiveness is not teeth-gritting determination to keep going no matter what. Sheer willpower to overlook or minimize an offense will never achieve forgiveness. Quite often, such an approach creates bitterness instead, especially when the other person fails to respond as desired.

Forgiveness is not merely excusing people who offend our personal preferences or who annoy us by their selfish choices, such as a friend who orders a pizza with everything on it when he knows you don't eat olives and mushrooms, or the obnoxious driver who cuts you off on the freeway. These may test our tolerance levels, but not our willingness to forgive.

What Forgiveness Is
While tolerance makes allowances, forgiveness releases a legitimate debt.

Throughout life there are many things we rightfully owe people; and there are things that we, in turn, expect from others. We owe love to God, others, and our enemies (Matthew 5:44; Mark 12:30-31). We owe honor to God, parents, and each other (1 Samuel 2:30; Romans 12:10; Ephesians 6:2). We owe obedience to God, employers, church leaders, and authorities (Deuteronomy 13:4; Romans 13:1-2; Ephesians 6:5; Hebrews 13:17), and depending on our position of authority, obedience is also due us. We owe faithfulness to God, our spouse, our friends, and others (Proverbs 3:3-4; 1 Corinthians 6:18-20), and we should expect faithfulness in return.

Yet though we know how we should treat others and how we want them to relate to us, we still fail. Sometimes we fail miserably, badly wounding—or being wounded by—others.

When Christ tells us to forgive, He is speaking to those who are most vulnerable—those who have, in some way, been violated. He knows that He speaks to people whose trust has been betrayed or who face humiliation. His words are intended for those whose character or reputation has been unjustly damaged, for the one whose life has been unfairly invaded and marred by the sin of others. And that is the difficulty of forgiveness—the offended person is affected by someone else's moral failure. Quite plainly, it is not fair. Yet, in the midst of pain and disillusionment, Christ says, "Forgive."

We must understand that Jesus is not minimizing the violations that maim lives. He is not questioning the authenticity of the offense and its harm. But at the point of trampled innocence, we are still told to forgive. We are told to release a legitimate debt. When we forgive, we guarantee that the offending person's violation will not be held against him.

Jesus never qualifies His statement. Whatever the failed obligation, whatever the violation, from first to last He says, "Forgive." And to make His point clear and to silence all exceptions, He adds, "as I have forgiven you."

Here there can be no argument. There is no debt of love and honor greater than what we owe Christ. There is no moral violation more profound than our disobedience to God. Yet He releases us. We are forgiven. And, as always, He says, "Follow Me."

The person who chooses to forgive acts contrary to any natural inclinations for immediate and personal justice, imitating Jesus' response to the unjust treatment He endured: "When they hurled their insults at him, he did not retaliate; when he suffered, he made no threats. Instead, he entrusted himself to him who judges justly" (1 Peter 2:23). Personal definitions of fairness are set aside. In fact, self is set aside altogether. The focus becomes Christ.

However real the offenses or injustices against us, however justified our hurt, we must view it all from the cross beams of Calvary. True forgiveness rises from a deep-rooted trust in Jesus Christ and in the values of His kingdom.

---

1. Think of an offender you are struggling to forgive or have had difficulty forgiving in the past. What is the debt that person owes you (or owed you)?

2. How were you injured by that person you struggle(d) to forgive?

3. What is your honest emotional reaction to the command to release your offender's debt—to say, in effect, "You don't owe me anything"?

4. Read the parable of the unmerciful servant in Matthew 18:23-35. Why was it so appalling for the servant to refuse to forgive his fellow servant's debt?

5. What kinds of debts has God forgiven you . . .

   ▪ In the past week?

   ▪ In the past year?

   ▪ In the past twenty years?

   ▪ When you became a Christian?

6. James wrote, "Whoever keeps the whole law and yet stumbles at just one point is guilty of breaking all of it" (James 2:10). How does this add to your understanding of how much you've been forgiven?

7. Read the parable of the Pharisee and the tax collector in Luke 18:9-14. When we withhold forgiveness, which man are we most like? Why?

8. Are any of the following true of the way you tend to forgive?

    ☐ I forgive the "little" sins but not the big ones.
    ☐ I forgive once or twice, but three strikes and you're out.
    ☐ I forgive, but I'd really rather not.
    ☐ I forgive only after the person has shown that he's got his act together.
    ☐ I forgive, but I sometimes remind the person of the sin when I'm trying to make a point.
    ☐ I forgive, but I want others to know what the person did to me.
    ☐ I forgive, but I never quite love the person as much again.

9. a. Colossians 3:13 says, "Forgive as the Lord forgave you." What is God's forgiveness like?

    ▪ Jeremiah 31:34

    ▪ John 3:16

- Romans 4:7-8

- Romans 5:8

- 1 John 1:9

b. As you looked up the preceding verses, did you see any ways in which your forgiveness should become more like God's? If so, how do you need to change?

10. a. We read in 2 Corinthians 5:15, "[Jesus] died for all, that those who live should no longer live for themselves but for him who died for them and was raised again." Why is forgiving difficult if you are living for yourself?

b. How might living for Jesus make forgiving easier?

11. Reflect on the author's last statement: "True forgiveness rises from a deep-rooted trust in Jesus Christ and in the values of His kingdom." Why is trust in Jesus and His teachings necessary before we can forgive?

Must We Forgive?

It is clear that God desires, commands, and expects us to be forgiving. But, as with so much of life, we are faced with choices. We can either say "I will" or "I won't"—it's up to us.

The person who decides against forgiveness, focusing instead on his own hurts and injustices, will reap severe consequences. Unforgiving people often live in a system of weights and balances, efforts and paybacks. In such a system, when an offense occurs, the guilty person comes under scrutiny and his behavior is closely watched. In a relationship of this sort, there is rarely enough behavioral change to satisfy the unforgiving person. The debt caused by the offense is never completely paid off. The offended person will always detect a mistake, will always find a reason to put off restoration.

Because the unforgiving person focuses upon the debt owed him, he is incapable of extending grace and forgiveness to the person who wronged him. Not surprisingly, he does not find the forgiveness and mercy of God satisfying. Unforgiveness erects a barrier to receiving God's forgiveness, cripples personal relationships, and warps a person's understanding of his own worth.

Jesus' model prayer for His disciples in Matthew 6 includes these oft-repeated words: "Forgive us our debts, as we also have forgiven our debtors" (verse 12). Christ develops this idea at the conclusion of the prayer by saying, "For if you forgive men when they sin against you, your heavenly Father will also forgive you. But if you do not forgive men their sins, your Father will not forgive your sins" (verses 14-15). Jesus' words echo the same warning He gave in the tale of the unmerciful servant. Unforgiving people are consumed with their own circumstances and feelings. The sad result is an arrogant denial of God's mercy, trivializing God's own great sacrifice. Their sense of personal wrong (however warranted) so fills their vision that they cannot see beyond it to the cross. Unforgiving people cannot be truly contrite before God in response to their own sins.

12. Mark 11:25 says, "When you stand praying, if you hold anything against anyone, forgive him, so that your Father in heaven may forgive you your sins." Why do you think unforgiveness hinders our fellowship with God?

13. Think of a bitter person you have known. What results of unforgiveness do you see in that person's life?

Back at the Cross

Christ refused to give in to natural inclinations and retaliate against His accusers. He leads the way by taking us back to the cross. There, nothing is ever the same; human relationships are transformed into divine interactions because Jesus always stands between. He stands between me and God, bringing together two who were estranged into a loving friendship. He stands between the new me and the old, enabling me to live by divine power a life of goodness that was otherwise impossible; and He stands between me and others, handing me the opportunity to live beyond myself in love . . . and forgiveness.

14. As Jesus was being crucified, He said, "Father, forgive them, for they do not know what they are doing" (Luke 23:34). How does Jesus' example help you to forgive those who have sinned against you?

15. How is love related to forgiveness?

16. Choose and complete one of the following exercises (a or b):

   a. Think about a situation in which you are struggling to forgive someone. Why is it difficult for you to forgive this person? What is your next step toward forgiving this person?

   b. Think about someone you know who is bitter toward another person. What could you share with this person to help him or her forgive?

Parting Thought

Never in the Word of God will you find that any crime is too great to forgive.

—Ruth Collins Server, "The Freedom of Forgiveness," Issue 34

7

Dealing with Conflict

Conflict is inevitable. Misunderstandings or selfish actions can lead to hurt feelings. A crack appears in a relationship—a crack that can widen into an unbreachable chasm if it is left unattended. Conflict can damage or even kill relationships.

1. Which of these statements is closest to the way you generally react to conflict?

    ☐ It's not important enough to bring up and risk ruining our relationship, so I'll forget it.
    ☐ Someday I might say something about it, but I'll just wait and see if it might resolve itself first.
    ☐ I want to talk about it. Christ can help us resolve our conflict.
    ☐ There's no way to resolve this conflict, so why try?

As followers of Jesus, we do not have the option of leaving conflicts unresolved. Paul wrote in Romans 12:18, "If it is possible, as far as it depends on you, live at peace with everyone." That takes conflict resolution.

In the following article entitled "**She's My Enemy, and I (a. Love, b. Hate, c. Ignore, d. Other) Her**" by Barbara Tetlow Beevers (excerpted from Issue 64), the author tells the story of a difficult relationship and how she attempted to respond in a biblical manner.

D When a Relationship Turns Sour

My husband and I had been welcomed into the fellowship of a small church. For many months we enjoyed rather ideal relationships there. But suddenly, a woman who at first had been very friendly turned against me with criticism and faultfinding. I went to her and tried to explain that I had not done the things she accused me of. Certainly I had not meant to hurt her feelings.

She didn't believe me. She persisted in thinking that I had wronged her. It seemed as if she *wanted* to find faults in me to complain about.

Eventually I realized this was not a misunderstanding I could clear up.

Once, fortified with hours of prayer and Bible study, I phoned her. "The Sunday school lesson was about reconciliation. Could we get together and talk about it?" Not only did she turn me down, but weeks later, when I greeted her after church, she said in a mocking tone, "How are you doing in your reconciliation efforts?"

It was hard to admit that this woman hated me. I tend to like everybody and I try to please. But after trying for three years to win her over, I'm ready to admit that I have an enemy.

Webster's New Collegiate Dictionary says an enemy is "one hostile to another; one who seeks the overthrow or failure of that to which he is opposed." So an enemy is not just someone I dislike. *My* feelings are not the determining factor. *Hers* are. And her feelings are not simple dislike, but hatred strong enough to seek my downfall. That's the kind of person Jesus tells us to love.

2.   What did Barbara do right when she perceived a rift between her and the other woman?

3. The following two passages in Matthew talk about what to do when we have a conflict. Based on these verses, who is to take the initiative to resolve a conflict, no matter who has been offended?

    If you are offering your gift at the altar and there remember that your brother has something against you, leave your gift there in front of the altar. First go and be reconciled to your brother; then come and offer your gift. (Matthew 5:23-24)

    If your brother sins against you, go and show him his fault, just between the two of you. If he listens to you, you have won your brother over. (Matthew 18:15)

4. Read Matthew 7:3-5. What do we need to do before we approach someone in order to resolve a conflict?

5. Read Romans 12:18. Are we responsible to resolve every conflict? Why or why not?

6. Read Matthew 18:16-17. What biblical steps toward resolving conflict were not discussed in the article?

D How Do You Love an Enemy?

How can I obey Jesus' command to love her? So far, I have found four ways.

1. I must forgive her unconditionally and repeatedly. I can truthfully say that I forgive this woman. But it hasn't been a once-and-for-all kind of forgiveness. Often another person will hear what my enemy has said or done and then sympathize or urge me to seek reconciliation. Each time the subject comes up, my disappointment and hurt come back, and I must deal with my feelings all over again. I've asked God to help me with my emotions, and He has—over and over again.

Many times she has seemed to have a change of heart, and I have thought my prayers were answered. She smiles or speaks a pleasant word to me, and I respond eagerly, only to have her deliver a barb that smarts for days.

But it's not just the past I have to deal with. Today I am more afraid of what she *will* do than angry about what she *has* done. Sometimes I see her at the shopping center and I feel a stab of apprehension. What will she say? How will I respond? I have learned that forgiveness may not come easily, but it must come *repeatedly.*

7. a. What situations tend to reawaken your anger toward someone who has injured you?

b. What helps you to let go of your anger when these situations arise?

2. I must look to Scripture for God's evaluation of the situation and for comfort. It is possible that some of her criticisms are true. When she interrupted a Bible study by saying, "How can you teach when you don't love people?" I was speechless. Others defended me, but I went home and asked the Lord if what she had said was true. The Lord reassured me that her words were not His vehicle of correction this time as I read the words of Isaiah, "If anyone does attack you, it will not be my doing" (54:15).

I've decided to follow some good advice from a friend. "Don't let criticism put you in a defensive mode," she said. "Keep on getting your plans from the Lord." That means that I don't let my enemy define my ministry or let her criticisms control my schedule.

God's Word has been like salve on my wounds. Words I had seen but not felt before have come alive with meaning. I know more of what the prophets felt when they were rejected, how Jesus felt when He was betrayed. And I have experienced God's comfort.

8. Has an enemy, or even someone who is angry with you, ever spoken words that you needed to hear? If so, what were they?

9. Read the story of Manasseh in 2 Chronicles 33:10-13. What did God do to get Manasseh's attention when he failed to listen to Him?

10. How can you discern whether a message from an enemy is really a message from God?

11. What Scriptures have comforted you after an enemy (or even a friend) attacks?

3. I must *actively* obey Jesus' command to love an enemy. The first action is prayer: "Pray for those who persecute you" (Matthew 5:44). I have found it fairly easy to pray for my enemy because it bothers me so much to *have* an enemy. I ask the Lord to bring her to repentance for the anger and bitterness she shows to others but does not admit to herself. I pray, "Search me, O God, and know my heart. . . . See if there is any offensive way in me" (Psalm 139:23-24). I pray this for her as well as for myself. I picture her receiving refreshment from the Lord as a result of repentance (Acts 3:19). Again and again I ask God for the power to love her and the power to forgive her.

Romans 12:14-21 has guided me through this whole process. Verses 14 and 17 have kept me from responding to her cutting remarks with remarks of my own ("Bless those who persecute you; bless and do not curse. Do not repay anyone evil for evil").

I also ask God to reveal specific ways that I can act toward her. Verse 20 says: "If your enemy is hungry, feed him; if he is thirsty, give him something to drink." My enemy is not physically hungry or thirsty, but she is hungry for praise. So I search for opportunities to give her a sincere compliment. Luke 6:35 also says to look for ways to do good and be kind to your enemy. I'm not often tempted to be unkind or to hurt her; I just want to avoid her. Still, Jesus says to take the initiative in approaching her. Do good. Be kind.

How can I minister to someone who hurts me? I want to do good to her, but when I see her, my guard is up. It's like trying to pet a porcupine. Each time I reach out, I get another wound.

I find comfort in knowing that Jesus experienced this guardedness too: "Jesus would not entrust himself to them, . . . for he knew what was in a man" (John 2:24-25). Yet Jesus spoke about the necessity of ignoring pain in order to serve others. He said, "If someone strikes you on one cheek, turn to him the other also" (Luke 6:29). He knew it would hurt, but He did it anyway. It was His way of trying to salvage the hating person.

12. Think of someone who might qualify as an "enemy" in your life right now. What can you pray for him or her?

13. a. Romans 12:14,17-21 lists a number of do's and dont's regarding how we treat our enemies. List them below.

Do	Don't

b. Which of the "do's" is most difficult for you? Why?

c. Which of the "dont's" is most tempting? Why?

14. a. What are some ways in which you could do good to your enemy?

b. What fears do you have about doing this?

c. How do Romans 12:14-21 and Luke 6:27-29 speak to those fears?

4. Finally, I refuse to hate her or wish her ill. Although I cannot escape having an enemy, I am determined not to *be* an enemy. Receiving hatred has been hard. But with God's help I can keep it from settling in my heart.

Sometimes the psalmists prayed that calamity would fall on their enemies. I guess that shows how human they were. But it wasn't Jesus' style, and I don't want it to be mine.

The world will not see the Father's unconditional love for them unless we Christians model it. No matter who is opposing me, I want to keep reaching out, to keep hoping for reconciliation. But even if reconciliation never comes, I can win a different kind of victory. I can obey my Lord and honor Jesus' name by loving my enemy.

15. Study Luke 6:35-36. What two reasons does Jesus give for loving and doing good to our enemies?

    ▪

    ▪

16. One commentator says being "sons of the Most High" means being like God. How can you be like Him in the way you treat your enemy?

17. a. Read Hebrews 12:2-3. What does the writer say will give us courage when we are mistreated?

b. Think about how Jesus was treated during the last hours of His life and about how He reacted. What can you learn from Him about the Christlike way to respond to mistreatment?

Parting Thought

God wants me to love my enemies in the same way He loved His enemies: He died for them.

—Roy Anthony Borges, "Love Your Enemies," Issue 107

8

Putting It All Together

When we study the Bible, we often learn potentially life-changing lessons. But the demands and concerns of daily life can break in, and we fail to act on or even remember those lessons. In this session, we will review some of the principles we learned in this study and further consider how God wants to see those principles at work in our lives. Then we will look at a few final passages about the kinds of relationships God intends us to enjoy.

It may be most beneficial to spread your work on this session over several days, focusing on the review of one or two sessions each day.

Sessions One and Two: Learning to Love, Parts One and Two

1. Review what you learned about love in the first two sessions. How would you describe a loving person? How does a loving person think about others and treat them? How does he respond to people who "rub him the wrong way"?

2. When we live a life of love, it affects how we relate to people in all kinds of situations. Choose three of the scenarios below and describe how a loving person might respond.

- Your spouse or roommate forgets to pick up an ingredient you need in order to cook dinner.
- In a hurry to get to an appointment, you have just a few minutes to stop for gas. A new cashier makes mistake after mistake, and precious time ticks away.
- The women in your small group begin talking about how much they like the new pastor's wife. But someone you know who went to her last church warned you that she is controlling and manipulative.
- A driver cuts you off on the freeway.
- Your small group is deciding what to study. You and the other couples are excited about a new book on marriage, but the singles in your group look downcast when it comes up.
- You've been trying to conceive for seven years, and a newly-wed couple in your small group announces that they're expecting.
- A coworker makes a careless mistake that costs you an important client.
- A child in your Sunday school class continually misbehaves, disrupting the class.
- Your mother-in-law makes an insulting comment about you at a large family gathering.

3. Have you become a better "lover" since studying sessions one and two? If so, how?

4.   Which idea from these two sessions would you most like to remember and apply? Why?

Session Three: Putting Others First

5. a. List the five questions Howard Baker says we can ask ourselves in order to determine if we are relating to others humbly.

   ■

   ■

   ■

   ■

   ■

   b. What have you learned about yourself by asking these questions?

6.   Which idea from this session would you most like to remember and apply? Why?

Session Four: Caring for Christians

7. Look back at the definition of fellowship you wrote at the beginning of session four. Does that still accurately represent your opinion? If not, how would you now define Christian fellowship?

8. a. In question twenty-three, part a, of session four, which area of fellowship did you check? Check it again here.

   ☐ Sharpening
   ☐ Encouraging
   ☐ Stimulating
   ☐ Defending

   b. What progress have you made in this area since working on this session?

   c. In the next six months, what further progress would you like to see in your life in this area?

Session Five: Building Close Friendships

9. a. Think of one of your closest friends (not your spouse). Write his or her name here.

   b. What are the strengths of this friendship?

c. In what areas would you like to see the friendship grow and deepen?

d. Which ideas from this study would most help you deepen that friendship?

Session Six: Learning to Forgive

10. a. Since studying this session, what opportunities have you had to forgive others?

b. What did you find was most difficult about forgiving?

c. Which Scriptures from the session spoke to the difficulties you faced?

11. Spend some time in prayer, asking God to reveal if there is anyone in your life you still need to forgive. If there is, ask God to help you take the next step toward forgiving.

Session Seven: Dealing with Conflict

12. a. Read what Jesus said about how we are to treat our enemies:

> "You have heard that it was said, 'Eye for eye, and tooth for tooth.' But I tell you, Do not resist an evil person. If someone strikes you on the right cheek, turn to him the other also. And if someone wants to sue you and take your tunic, let him have your cloak as well. If someone forces you to go one mile, go with him two miles. . . .
>
> "You have heard that it was said, 'Love your neighbor and hate your enemy.' But I tell you: Love your enemies and pray for those who persecute you, that you may be sons of your Father in heaven. He causes his sun to rise on the evil and the good, and sends rain on the righteous and the unrighteous. If you love those who love you, what reward will you get? Are not even the tax collectors doing that? And if you greet only your brothers, what are you doing more than others? Do not even pagans do that? Be perfect, therefore, as your heavenly Father is perfect." (Matthew 5:38-48)

b. If we retaliate when someone strikes us, how does it affect the following?

- The relationship

- Our emotional life

- Our spiritual life

c. What happens when we turn the other cheek instead?

13. Why is it so difficult not to retaliate when we are attacked?

14. What do you think Jesus meant when He said we will be children of the Father if we love our enemies?

15. How does loving and praying for our enemies bring glory to God?

16. What principle or Scripture passage from this session do you most want to remember and apply? Why?

GUIDELINES FOR GODLY RELATIONSHIPS

17. a. The New Testament is filled with commands about how we are to treat others. Read the following Scriptures, underlining the attitudes we are to have and the actions we are to take toward other people.

    __ John 15:17—"This is my command: Love each other."
    __ Romans 12:10—"Be devoted to one another in brotherly love. Honor one another above yourselves."
    __ Romans 12:16—"Live in harmony with one another."
    __ Romans 14:13—"Stop passing judgment on one another."
    __ Romans 15:7—"Accept one another . . . just as Christ accepted you, in order to bring praise to God."

__ 1 Corinthians 1:10—"Agree with one another so that there may be no divisions among you and that you may be perfectly united in mind and thought."

__ Galatians 5:13—"Serve one another in love."

__ Ephesians 4:2—"Be completely humble and gentle; be patient, bearing with one another in love."

__ Ephesians 5:21—"Submit to one another out of reverence for Christ."

__ Colossians 3:9—"Do not lie to each other, since you have taken off your old self with its practices."

__ 1 Thessalonians 5:11—"Encourage one another and build each other up."

__ 1 Thessalonians 5:15—"Make sure that nobody pays back wrong for wrong, but always try to be kind to each other and to everyone else."

__ Hebrews 10:24—"Let us consider how we may spur one another on toward love and good deeds."

__ James 4:11—"Brothers, do not slander one another. Anyone who speaks against his brother or judges him speaks against the law and judges it."

__ James 5:9—"Don't grumble against each other, brothers, or you will be judged."

__ James 5:16—"Confess your sins to each other and pray for each other so that you may be healed."

__ 1 Peter 4:9—"Offer hospitality to one another without grumbling."

__ 1 Peter 5:5—"Young men, in the same way be submissive to those who are older. All of you, clothe yourselves with humility toward one another, because, 'God opposes the proud but gives grace to the humble.'"

b. These instructions were intended to apply to how believers interact with other believers. Write a "U" next to the ones that you think also apply to how we treat unbelievers.

c. From the preceeding above, what new thoughts did you gain about relating in a godly way to other people?

d. Circle the verse that you would most like to practice more consistently.

18. a. Look back over everything you've written in this session. What *one* change in your life would you most like to see as a result of working through this study guide?

b. Tell a friend how you would like to respond to what God is saying to you through this study. Ask your friend to pray for you and to ask you occasionally about your progress in this area.

More help from DISCIPLESHIP JOURNAL for maturing in Christ and dealing with the issues of life.

Beating Busyness

Identify and tackle stressful issues in your life through articles, questions, quotes, Scripture, and related exercises in this *Discipleship Journal* Bible study.

Beating Busyness
(Adam R. Holz) $6

Becoming More Like Jesus

Becoming like Jesus is a process, not learning a list of rules. Based on excerpts from top *Discipleship Journal* articles, this study will develop His character in you as you evaluate your life, understand Jesus' teachings on character, and live them out.

Becoming More Like Jesus
(Michael M. Smith) $6

Following God in Tough Times

Even when we feel imprisoned by life's difficult circumstances, God gives us freedom to choose how we'll respond. Learn how to accept and gain perspective of tough times as you move from survival to service.

Following God in Tough Times
(Michael M. Smith) $6

Growing Deeper with God

Do you deeply desire to be intimate with God? Interact with Him on a personal level as you uncover the Father's heart through articles, questions, quotes, Scripture, and related exercises.

Growing Deeper with God
(Susan Nikaido) $6

Get your copies today at your local bookstore, through our website, or by calling (800) 366-7788. Ask for offer **#6019** or a FREE catalog of NavPress resources.

NAVPRESS

BRINGING TRUTH TO LIFE
www.navpress.com

Prices subject to change